Hornets & Hippos:

How to Use Imagination, Mindfulness, and Brain Science to Decrease Fear and Anger and Reach Your Goals

MARGARET ANN JESSOP, PsyD

This workbook is not a substitute for mental health care. It is designed to provide information and suggested activities for a parent and child to work on together. If you are concerned that you are experiencing mental health difficulties, please seek an in-person evaluation from a licensed professional.

Hornets & Hippos: How to Use Imagination, Mindfulness, and Brain Science to Decrease Fear and Anger and Reach Your Goals/Margaret Ann Jessop, PsyD

ISBN-13: 978-1974550227
ISBN-10: 1974550222

Published by CreateSpace

For information and permission to reproduce selections or worksheets from this book, please contact Dr. Jessop via email at meganajessop@gmail.com or by phone 574-258-6300 (ext. 5).
Thank you for your interest.

You can also visit the Hornets and Hippos website where you can download full-size copies of some of the worksheets in this workbook, and where you can also add your own hornet and hippo pictures to the "What's in Your Head Gallery." You can also find out about upcoming events at: www.hornets-and-hippos.com.

Illustrations, book layout, and cover design by Karyn Lewis Illustration
www.karynlewis.com
Editing by Editing Genie
www.editing-genie.com

ACKNOWLEDGMENTS

For All This I Am Grateful

Hornets & Hippos has been a long and rewarding project, and I am grateful to have so many supportive people I need to thank. First, I want to thank my writing group members, Karyn Lewis Bonfiglio, Alison Levy, and Alexa Kaufhold. I look forward to meetings full of creative ideas and sound edits. You ladies have kept me on my path, and I am thankful. A special thanks to Karyn for not only providing extra editing, but for your willingness to take on the art and really bring my characters alive. I love my Buddha Hippo! Second, I want to thank my colleagues, Elly Wynia, Donna Voor, Katy Maxwell, and Leslye Runkle. I have needed your constant encouragement and clinical sounding boards while coming up with Hornets & Hippos. Also, thank you Elly for your keen eye during your South Africa safari where you found the hippo with the bird on his back that I use in my hippo storytelling. That was synchronicity in play. Third, there is my partner in presentations, Debbie Raybold. Thank you for reading a 90-page book dropped on your desk by a stranger; thank you for seeing the way it could become more; and thank you for your love and attention as the project continues to grow. Then there are the people who inspire my creativity. April Pulley Sayre, I still remember the first time I saw you present, and I knew that was what I wanted to do. I love your spirit. All the children I have the pleasure of working with also inspire me. You are all so brave to work on understanding yourselves better, and it is with you I find my own inspiration. Finally I am grateful for my family, Colin, Hadley and Calum. Thank you for all the times you were patient with me when I was busy writing on our car rides to the beach, and the Thursday nights I was out at writing group. Thanks for your love and support.

TABLE OF CONTENTS

AUTHOR'S NOTE

I started my work with children in 1990 right after college, teaching at Duck's Nest Preschool in Berkeley, California. The experience was incredible, both in getting to know all the little people, and being entrusted with their care. I still have vivid memories of talking on pretend phones; playing with warm, homemade play dough; and helping put children to sleep at nap time, each with their own special lovey in their arms. There were scary moments too, like when one child 'walked the plank' right off the climbing structure; or when two kids went missing. We found the missing ones. They were just out of sight in a closet, using their imaginations, which, at that moment, were made stronger by playing in the dark. After ice and empathy, our plank-walker was also okay; but I was amazed by just how powerful their imaginations were. Walking a plank was like stepping off into imagination—no fear, just possibilities.

Teaching led me back to school—developmental psychology for two years, and then a doctoral program where I trained to become a clinician. Specializing in anxiety, I have continued to work in private practice with children and parents since 2000.

This workbook combines both clinical knowledge of anxiety and children's natural ability to use their imagination. It also gives the reader an understanding of some of the ways the brain works, as well as skills from the growing field of mindfulness. Hornets and Hippos will help normalize anxiety while engaging creativity. This approach helps children get back to the business of being children, leaving their fears behind so that they can continue to walk off imaginary planks and explore the world ahead of them. I hope you enjoy Hornets & Hippos along with them. You might find it helps you with your anxiety, too.

INTRODUCTION

Hornets & Hippos

Your brain is a buzzing bundle of endless abilities. It warns you to react to danger. It helps you pay attention, learn new things, and remember what you have learned. It connectes you to others, and even builds thoughts and connections unique only to you. Creating new thoughts can also be called *using your imagination*, and it is one of your most powerful learning tools.

While you are young, your imagination is much stronger than a grownup's imagination. This is why I have written this book for you. I have developed a way for you to use your powerful imagination, and your brain's amazing abilities, to keep you feeling good and moving toward your goals.

In this workbook you will use your imagination and your ability to learn new things to understand what happens to you when you get scared and angry. You will learn about brain science and the ways your brain works to keep you alive. Even though it is normal to get scared or angry, sometimes this reaction can be so strong that it overpowers the brain. When this happens, it can be hard to relax, stay connected to others, learn, and have fun. Our brains can get stuck in this mode, limiting other brain abilities.

You will also get a chance to learn and practice mindfulness. Mindfulness is the practice of focused attention. You could think of mindfulness as shining a flashlight on a spot, a thought, or a moment, and really paying attention to where the light is shining. In this workbook you will be introduced to a number of mindful activities as well as guided mindful practices, which are referred to as **mindful moments**. You will be guided to relax your body and slow down your thoughts while listening to a story, or focusing on your breath. Mindful practices will help you achieve your goals. If you struggle with negative thoughts, mindful practice can help you grow positive ones. And don't worry if you haven't done anything like this before. You will learn that even on your busiest days, it's not only easy to make time for mindful moments, but enjoyable, too.

Are you ready to learn the skills you need to use your brain's abilities to tackle the things that make you fearful or angry? Let's get started.

In this workbook you will explore:

• How to use your imagination and your ability to learn new things to understand what happens when you are scared or angry. You will also learn to recogonize when you are calm, and how gathering information can help you become emotionally balanced.

• Understand why getting scared and angry are normal—and sometimes very helpful feelings—and why feeling calm helps us pay attention, stay connected, and learn.

• How movement and breathing help calm your mind and body.

• Practice mindfulness and discover how you can use this skill to calm fear and anger.

• Discover just how amazing you and your brain are. You will be able to keep fear and anger away—until you need them.

Imagine Your Hornet and Hippo

So what do hornets and hippos have to do with feeling scared, angry, paying attention, and learning? Let's use your imagination to find out. I am giving you a hornet of your very own, and I want you to pretend that it lives in your brain. That's right, you now have a little hornet that looks a lot like a bumblebee living in your brain.

Here is how I picture the hornet in my brain:

Picture what yours might look like. Remember you have an incredible imagination. You can close your eyes if this helps you see your hornet.

Now let's go bigger—much bigger—and imagine you have a hippo in your brain, too. (Close your eyes again if you are having trouble imagining the hippo.)

Once you have the hippo in sight, see if you can fit in a tree or even a big pond around it. Is your brain making room for all these things? It's like you are creating your very own African plain right there in your head!

How are you doing? Can you see them yet? What does your hornet look like? Did you figure out how to fit your hippo inside your brain?

If you can imagine your own hornet and hippo, then you are ready to move on to chapter one. If you like, use the picture of a head on the next page to draw your hornet and hippo and any other details your imagination created.

What's in Your Head?

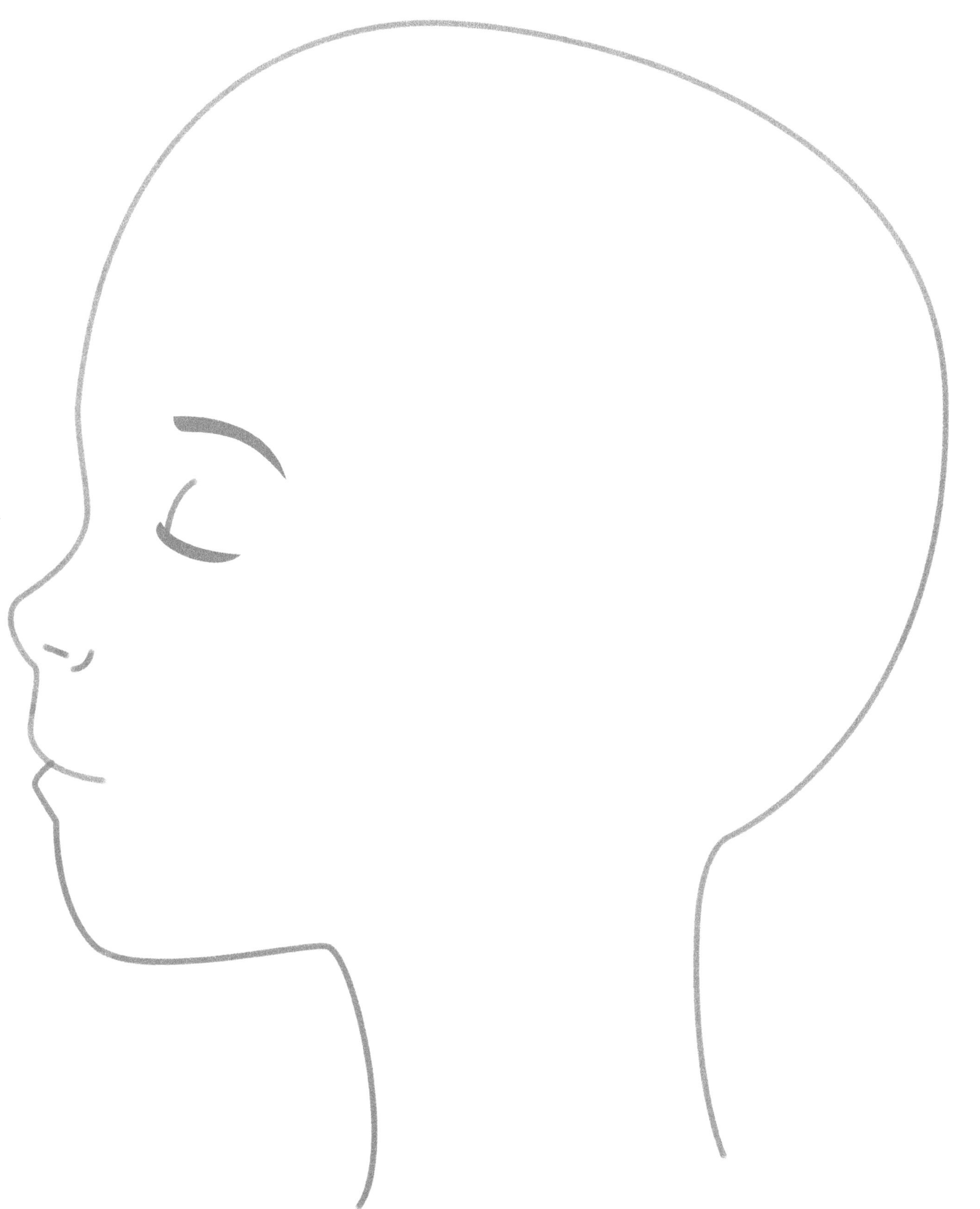

CHAPTER ONE

Using Your Hornet-Brain

Have you ever seen a real, live hornet? If you have, you might have felt afraid; or maybe you were curious about what the little guy could do. If you haven't seen one, hornets are small insects similar to bees, and they are very good at reacting when danger threatens their hive.

For example, if an animal gets too close, or takes too much interest in their hive, the hornets will buzz around and try to sting anything nearby. In short, if there is a problem, they react!

Your brain has a similar ability. Let's call it your **hornet-brain**. This is a small part of your brain that you use to help identify and react to trouble of any kind.*

Sometimes this part of the brain is called the *alarm bell*, but it reacts more like a hornet than a bell. Bells ring, but hornets buzz around or sting. In other words, hornets fly or fight for their life. In the next chapter, we'll see how this works.

But first—do you see the little hornet at the bottom of this page? Throughout this workbook, Hornet Talk sections (and Hippo Talk sections, too!), will help you understand the brain science behind Hornets & Hippos.

Once you have read the Hornet Talk section below, on the next page see if you can find the amygdala inside the head and brain illustration that I have included for you. When you do, color it in. You might have to look really hard, because the amygdala is very small. See if you can color in your whole brain.

Finally, if you are curious (like me!) and you would like to know what the other parts of your brain do, I have included a glossary with more information for you to refer to on the back of the worksheet.

* HORNET TALK

"The part of the brain that we are calling the hornet is called the **amygdala**, and you have one on each side of your brain."

Color Your Brain

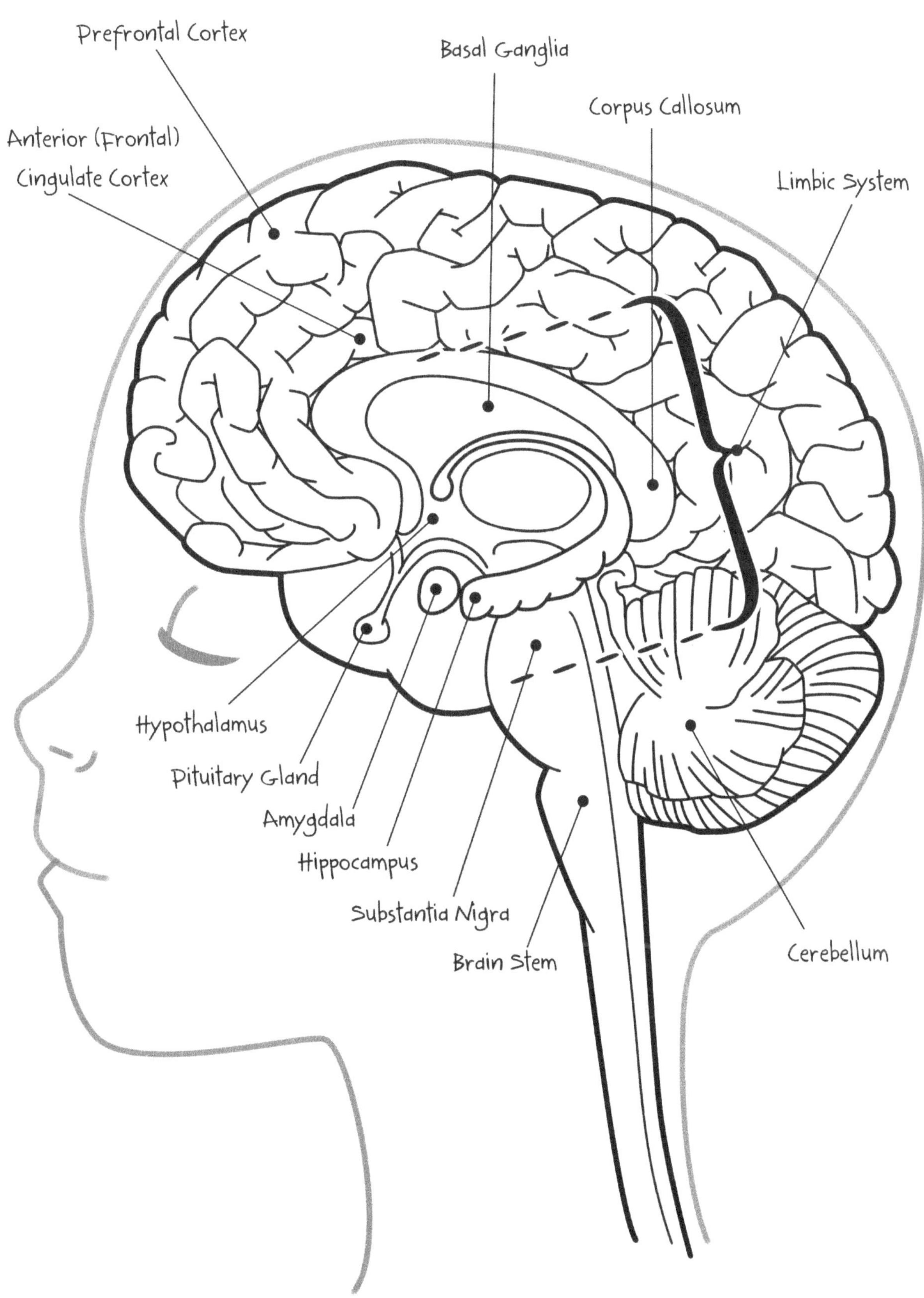

Color Your Brain Definitions

Amygdala is the part of the brain where the fight-or-flight response is initiated—what this workbook calls the "Hornet."

Anterior (frontal) Cingulate Cortex helps with regulating decision making, impulse control and emotions.

Basal Ganglia is a group of structures that help start movement, balance, eye movement, and keeping your posture.

Brain Stem helps monitor breathing, heart rate, and blood pressure through the control of these automatic functions.

Cerebellum regulates motor behavior and it monitors automatic movements; also likely a part of attention and learning.

Corpus Callosum connects the right and left sides of the brain.

Hippocampus is the part of the brain that takes in the context of the situation around us and builds memories—what this workbook calls the "Hippo."

Hypothalamus regulates hunger, thirst, and body temperature.

Limbic System is a group of brain structures that help process and regulate emotions and memory. The hornet and hippo are a part of the limbic system.

Pituitary Gland helps regulate growth and reproduction.

Prefrontal Cortex is the part of the brain behind the forehead where we plan and make decisions.

Substantia Nigra is part of the Basal Ganglia and helps with moving your body.

CHAPTER TWO

You Are in Danger: Hornet to the Rescue

If you've ever been scared or angry, you have used your hornet. Fearful feelings often begin when you are in danger, or when you imagine or remember a threatening or frightening situation.

It's not just your thoughts that can cause fear or anger, however. Sensations that you experience through your five senses—sight, hearing, smell, touch, and taste—can also trigger this response.

For example, you might see an unfamiliar face, or hear a loud noise. You might smell something burning. Perhaps you eat something that tastes strange, and you worry you might throw up. Or maybe something touches your skin and you feel it could harm you. These stimuli send messages straight to your brain, which, in turn, sends a string of signals to the rest of your body that danger is near. But how does this work? To see how anger and fear might play out in your brain, let's examine the following steps in three, very different examples.

1) Something touches your skin that alarms you.

Step One: You are busy playing and using your imagination when…

Step Two: You feel something brush the skin on your arm.

Step Three: You think, *Something is biting my arm, and this could hurt me.*

Step Four: You get a gut feeling something isn't right and think, *I could be in danger.*

Step Five: Your body reacts. Your heart starts to race, and your breath becomes short.

Step Six: You fearfully shake your arm or swat at the spot where you felt the inital touch. You might feel mad that this happened.

2) You are nauseous and worry you will throw up at school.

Step One: At school, your stomach is very upset and you spend the day feeling like you are going to throw up.

Step Two: You go home that day and begin to feel better.

Step Three: The next morning as you get ready for school, you remember your tummy ache, and you worry that you will get sick at school.

Step Four: In class you can't concentrate because you're so worried you will throw up, and you think that going home will solve the problem.

Step Five: You're afraid to face your friends at school because you feel sure that if you get sick, they will think negative things about you.

Step Six: You start to wonder if school itself is causing you to feel this way. Now you want to avoid school altogether, and you might even feel angry that you have to go.

3) It is night, and time to go to bed.

Step One: You are in your room and your parents have just put out most of the lights.

Step Two: You notice you can't see as much as you could with the lights on.

Step Three: You hear a noise, and you aren't sure what it is.

Step Four: Your amazing imagination kicks in and comes up with some scary ideas of what that noise was.

Step Five: Frightened by your imagination, you decide it would be wise to have your parents help you fall asleep. You might feel mad they want you to sleep on your own.

Step Six: The next night, you think about scary things before bed, and can't fall asleep without help from your parents.

In these examples, the information your senses take in travels through your nervous system to your brain, where your hornet registers the information as danger. Because your hornet's number-one job is to keep you safe, your body will stop everything to listen to this message.

Do you remember what happened in example number one? Alarmed by the feeling of something touching your skin—***BAM!*** You swatted the spot.

Now, if it had been a bug that was nibbling on you, you would have done a great job protecting yourself. If, however, it was not a bug but your brother, who was dangling your favorite stuffed animal on your arm; that touch-feeling might have made you overly fearful. Even though there was no real danger around, you might have spent a tremendous amount of energy swatting at thin air—or your brother.

In the second example, in which you equated school with throwing up, you avoided a location that you believed was dangerous, even though it was not. If school was truly making you feel sick, then avoiding it might help; but chances are school didn't make you feel sick, and now you are fearful of something that was actually good for you.

Finally in the bedtime example, with your ability to see diminished by lack of light in your room, your imagination did its amazing job and made up fearful situations even when you were perfectly safe in your bed.

Occasionally overreacting to something that is not dangerous is okay; but if you do it daily or multiple times a day, your body starts to get worn out. You are also missing out on lots of possible good experiences. This is not fair to you.

Since we started this workbook imagining we were on an African plain where hornets and hippos live, let's use our imagination to look at another example, and examine what happens when our hornet responds to danger.

Imagine we are on the edge of a pond in Africa. Let's pretend that a lioness is approaching. Can you picture the color of her fur and see her long tail? She looks hungry and you don't want to be her lunch. You need to get away fast! Running, you think, is the best plan of action. So your hornet sends a chemical message from your brain to your body and—*BAM!* You jump into survival mode.

Your body automatically reacts to the crisis. You might feel your breath get shallow or your heart race as your heart and lungs work to get more oxygen and blood to your body. Your hands might get warm or sweaty, or you might feel sick to your stomach. Some people even feel they have to go to the bathroom to pee, or even poop. (Because your body is moving its energy to its arms and legs, it can't spend energy on digestion of your food; so it wants to purge your stomach [throwing up], or bladder [urination], or bowels [diarrhea].) Lastly, chemicals are redirecting blood from the middle of your body out to your arms and legs, giving them added energy.*

All of these reactions are happening to you because your hornet has been busy at work preparing your body to flee, or fight to survive.

Wow, is your body amazing or what? It can do all of this in just a matter of seconds. You are an incredible survivor!

* HORNET TALK

"Your ability to react this way is called the *fight-or-flight response*. Scientists believe that having this ability has kept us alive and able to survive many dangers. One of the chemicals your body makes to help you respond is called **cortisol**, and it is also referred to as a stress hormone."

Ready to Survive the Challenge

People feel a number of things when they get scared. Here's a list of common sensations people experience. **Circle the ones that you have noticed**. As you look through the list below, remember these are normal feelings, which happen to help you survive.

Heart rate increases	Breathing changes
Have to go pee often	Have to go poop
Diarrhea	Upset stomach
Feel like throwing up	Throwing up
Lack of hunger	Wanting to eat all the time
Sweating	Trouble sleeping
Trouble paying attention	Not hearing very well
Can't remember very well	Pain in parts of your body
Can't stop looking for danger everywhere	Hearing things that are not there
Feel like passing out	Passing out

OTHER:

____

____

____

____

Activity: Mindful M.E.D.S.

We now know that our hornet brain helps us survive any danger or challenge, and that the fight-or-flight response has helped keep us alive for generations. But wouldn't it be nice to turn it off when you don't need it? This workbook will teach you several different ways to help you remain calm. But first, I want to give you my top four, best ways to turn off those feelings of fear and anger when you don't need them. I call these four aids, **M.E.D.S.**

1. MOVEMENT

Helps anxious and angry energy dissipate and bring us to rest.

If your body goes into hornet-mode, your arms and legs are ready to move. So choose an exercise or movement like marching, jumping, skipping, running, or dancing, and move for 2–5 minutes. Be sure to use both the right and left side of your body. Afterwards, your body will calm down much easier.

2. EXHALE

Helps turn on the parasympathetic (vagus) nervous system and calms us.

When we get scared we breathe short and fast. We want to reverse this and make our breaths long and slow. First, empty your lungs. Next, inhale while you or your parent count to four. Once your lungs are full, exhale as slowly as you can—to the count of six or seven seconds. See if you can make your exhale longer than your inhale. Keep repeating this conscious breathing for a minute or two. If your mind and your breath wander, that's okay; just come back to it.

3. Drinking Water

Helps the body know you are safe and ready to use your stomach.

When you drink fluids, your body responds as though no danger is present. Keep a water bottle nearby and sip throughout the day. (Parents, many schools will let your child have a water bottle at his or her desk, so be sure to ask to let your child do this.)

4. SQUAT SPOT

Squatting puts pressure on the vagus nerve in the heart and slows your heart rate.

The goal for this exercise is to squat down and put your arms around your knees, or steeple your hands together on top of your knees. If you are comfortable, stay there for a few minutes. This exercise will slow your heart rate, and help calm your body. Afterwards, be sure to slowly stand up or sit down in a chair to avoid feeling light-headed. If you are unable to squat, that's okay. Just bend at the waist and rest your hands on your knees—as much as your body will allow. This exercise can also be done while seated in a chair. With your feet resting on the floor, lean your torso onto your lap.

Practicing these activities daily will help you feel calmer and better able to access all of your brain's abilities. They will also help you to keep your hornet from running the show when it's not needed. At the end of the workbook (page 119), I have included a reminder sheet for you to hang up at home or give to your teachers. Over time, daily practice will make a significant difference in your ability to calm your body.

Mindful Moment:
Your Body Is Looking Out for You

It's amazing how your body looks out for you, isn't it? In the previous chapter, you learned how your brain releases the hormone cortisol when you are scared and stressed, and how it prepares you to get into fight-or-flight mode. Now it's time to learn about another important chemical that your body makes to heal from the dangerous or scary experience you've just gone through.

This chemical is **oxytocin***, which is sometimes called the "cuddle hormone," because you also make it when you get, or give, hugs. Once created, the cuddle hormone is released into your bloodstream and travels into the openings inside your heart to help it heal and stay healthy.

So, I'd like you to give yourself a hug with a mindfulness excercise I've created for you. I call this practice a *mindful moment*. To begin, find a comfortable spot either on a chair or on the floor. Take a moment to notice how your body feels. Make any needed adjustments until your body feels at peace.

Next, focus on your breath as it moves in and out. As you sit quietly, you might notice changes in how comfortable you feel. If at any time during this mindful practice you feel uncomfortable, adjust what you need to until you feel content.

Next find a point in the room to focus on. Or if you like, close your eyes and focus inside. Have a parent or other adult read the following paragraph to you. As you listen, your only job is to concentrate on your breath and observe where your thoughts take you. You will also be given a chance to sit quietly at the end of this story.

MINDFUL MOMENT: CUDDLE TIME

(Parent: Read slowly, pausing between each sentence.)

For this first mindful moment, I want you to think about someone you feel really comfortable with. It could even be a stuffed animal you love. Next, I want you to imagine that person or stuffed animal giving you a very big hug. Can you remember that sensation? Use your senses. Can you picture the person or the animal? What does their hair smell like? How does the fabric of their clothes feel on your skin? Can you remember the colors they wear? Focus on how the hug feels to you. Where do you feel it in your body? What emotions are you feeling? Is your body calm or uncomfortable? What is your heart doing? Can you notice your breath? Now is your chance to just sit and feel your hug. I invite you to stay with this hug for one to two minutes.

(Parent: Pause, then check in to see what your child noticed.)

Were you able to pause and notice how you felt? What was your experience like? Did you share it with the person who read to you? If not, take a few minutes to do so.

Remember that every time you get scared or angry your body is not only preparing you to be safe; but it is also caring for you, and trying to heal any distress you are experiencing. When your body is in fight-or-flight mode we sometimes call it feeling "stressed." But I want you to remember this reaction isn't all negative. Your body is activating your safety system, too.

Your body uses this safety system to help you reach a goal. That goal could be staying safe, or that goal could be doing something brand new. It could be accomplishing something specific—like doing well on a test, or playing a great game of soccer. It could even be helping you stay connected to your family and friends.

The more you are able to understand this hornet-brain system, the less you will experience your body's fight-or-flight response as negative; instead, you will see that is a positive force. The hornet-brain drives us towards our "stay safe" goals, and it pushes us towards one another, so we can get support from others, too.

* HORNET TALK

"The hormone oxytocin, which is also called the "cuddle hormone" by scientists, plays an important role in building trust with others, and bonding with our loved ones. It can even help us feel less depressed."

CHAPTER THREE

Hornets Build a Hive of Information

Does your hornet have a big hive, or a small one?

So you saw the lioness, and you ran away. Now you're safe and calm. You survived, but that was a close one! Even though the danger passed, your brain is still working to keep you safe in the future by not only remembering the event that just happened; but it builds a network of information around your hornet-brain that will enable you to react even faster to danger the next time. (This network is made up of brain cells called **neurons**, and your brain holds billions of neurons!) This means that each time you experience fight-or-flight mode, the stronger this network grows. Think about this network like a hornet's nest—each new event is added in much the same way hornets build their hive layer by layer. Over time, it's as though you're building a hive of information in your brain. Hornets don't need instruction to build their nests. It's a natural ability they're instinctively wired to do. Humans also don't need instruction on how to respond to, or remember, danger. We're born with this ability, just as hornets are born knowing how to construct their hives.

In fact, our brains recall dangerous experiences more easily than they remember positive ones.* Why is this? To survive, our brains are designed to hold onto any information that can hurt us. As a result, sometimes we focus more on our fearful thoughts than on our happier moments. Or to put it another way, it's like the danger-center in your brain is doing push-ups, making it stronger. When this happens, you can get more scared then you need to.

Has this ever happened to you? Let's use the worksheet on the next page to write down the things that are scaring you. First, I'd like you to identify your fear, and then describe what you are afraid might happen because of it. Next, write down what you would *really like to happen* if you could pick a *positive outcome* instead of a fearful one. This may sound a bit strange, but if you think about it, fear is pushing you towards a goal. It's as if your goal is hiding behind your hornet's nest. When we're calm, we can focus on achieving a desired outcome, such as staying safe or setting fear aside. Or perhaps you just want to do well in school. You might wish to make friends, or maybe you want to be brave enough to try something new.

Take your time filling out the worksheet as any fears show up. After awhile, you might notice it is fun to turn each fear into a positive goal. Moving your focus to a positive outcome feels so much better, and it will get easier with practice.

* HORNET TALK

"Your extra ability to remember scary events is called **negativity bias**. From a survival standpoint, memories of harmful events are valuable information. Therefore, the brain is wired to access them quickly to help us avoid danger in the future. Unfortunately it can also stress us out more than is needed to survive."

Your Fear Vs. Your Goal

Take a moment to think about the thing (or things) that scare you. In the column on the left, name the fear or worry that is bothering you. In the middle column, describe what you are afraid will happen because of this event or thing. In the final column, describe your real goal or the outcome you're excited about.

THE FEAR	THE FEARED OUTCOME	THE REAL GOAL
Phoebe is afraid of taking tests.	*She is afraid that if she doesn't do well, she will get in trouble and not be good enough. She is worried that she is not perfect.*	*She wants to do well on her test.*
YOUR FEAR	**YOUR FEARED OUTCOME**	**YOUR REAL GOAL**
1)		
2)		

Mindful Moment 2:
Fear-Free/Anger-Free Moment

So far in this workbook, we've been talking a lot about the brain and what happens when we get scared. For this mindful practice, I'd like you to let these thoughts go, and focus on a time in your life when you did not feel scared—a time you felt at peace.

Believe it or not you have been free from fear far more often than you have been scared. So let's get started, and remember what this feels like in your body. Find a comfortable spot either on a chair or the floor. Take a moment to notice how your body feels. Make any needed adjustments until your body feels at peace. Notice your breath as it moves in and out. As you sit quietly, you might notice changes in how comfortable you feel. If at any time during this mindful practice you feel uncomfortable, adjust what you need to until you feel content. Next, find a point in the room to focus on. Or if you like, close your eyes and focus inside. Have a parent or other adult read you the following paragraphs, which is an example of a fear-free moment that I have experienced. Your only job is to listen, breathe, and observe where your thoughts take you. When you are finished, you will be given a chance to sit quietly at the end, and think about your fear-free moment.

My Fear-Free Moment: The Beach

(Parent: Read slowly, pausing between each sentence.)

I remember going to the beach when I was a little girl. I can still see the beach in my mind, on the west coast of Northern California. I remember the light, tan color of the sand, and the steady rhythm of the crashing waves. Hungry seagulls roam the beach in search of food that someone left behind. I even remember the change in temperature from hot to cold as the sun and wind brush over my skin. The time of year I am thinking of is summer, and my whole family is there with me. As I explore the beach, the cool waves surge past my legs in a calming rhythm.

Today I still like the beach, no matter if it's on the east or west coast, or the coast of a huge lake. It's still a place I can go—or even just think about going to—and feel calm. Now I want you to remember a fear-free moment that you've experienced. It can be anything. Perhaps you too were on a beach with your family. Or maybe you remember a really fun day you had, or a day when you were with some of the people you feel most comfortable with. Your fear-free moment could have been a birthday or holiday your family celebrates. Remember the time of the year, the temperature, and who was with you. What details can you see? How do you know you weren't scared? What do you notice about your body when you remember your fear-free moment?

(Parent: Pause, then check in to see what your child noticed.)

On the next page, I'd like you to write down that memory. Try to include details from all of your senses. If you have a picture of that day, you can add that, too.

Your Mindful Fear-Free/Anger-Free Moment

____

____

____

____

____

____

____

Now that you have your fear-free memory down, I want you to notice how your body feels. What is your breath like? How is your heart beating? Notice your hands and your feet. What are they doing? Does your body feel warm, or some other temperature? What else do you notice about how your body feels? Take a moment and record your observations in the space below.

____

____

____

____

____

____

Were you able to describe a fear-free memory? How do you feel right now? I bet that any stress, anxiety, or fear that your body was experiencing before this mindful practice has lessened, or has even disappeared entirely. Isn't that cool? Your mind is so powerful, that just by remembering a positive memory, your brain can share that positive feeling with every part of you.

I hope you will remember how this works, because you can do this mindful practice anytime you want. You can use it before bed, or while you are riding in a bus or a car. You can even use this technique in your classroom as you get ready to take a test.

What you choose to think about will guide your body. And remember, you *can* choose what you think about. This is mindfulness. The practice of noticing your thoughts helps you achieve the feeling you are aiming for.

But wait, there is another reason to practice positive thoughts, too—but I need to explain a bit more before I tell you. So let's keep reading.

CHAPTER FOUR

Calming the Hornet

Now that you are feeling calm, I want to get back to working on one of your own problems—whatever it is that you are struggling with. In this chapter, we are going to look specifically at what is frightening you or worrying you, and find positive things associated with that problem to make you feel calm. That's right. I want you to take your fear, look it in the eye, and learn more about it! (This technique will work on feelings of anger, too. So, if your problem causes you more anger than fear, then focus on the problem that makes you angry.)

The more you know about your negative emotions, the more you will feel calm. Let us use Phoebe as an example. Remember, we learned in the *Fear Vs. Goal Worksheet* (page 33) that Phoebe had a fear of test-taking. To help Phoebe learn more about her fear, I would start by having Phoebe gather information about her tests. For example, I would ask Phoebe to tell me how many tests she had taken, and how well she had done on them. I would ask Phoebe how she feels after she finishes her exams, and how she feels when she studies well for them.

By gathering this information, we can usually find many good moments regarding test-taking. The goal is to **learn to focus on the positive details**, rather than focusing on the fear of a bad outcome.

Now let's have you try. Remember, we are looking for as much information as we can find. Use the worksheets on pages 43–46 to examine your fear or anger, and turn your new knowledge into a positive outcome.

Look Your Fear in the Eye!

Let's face the fear or anger that you are experiencing and gather more information about it. Write your responses to the questions listed below.

1) What is the fear or anger you are having trouble with?

2) How long have you been feeling this fear or anger?

3) Were you ever not scared of it?

4) How many days were you not scared of it? (If it was years, count up the days.) You might be surprised by how many days you weren't afraid of it.

5) Was there a time you were not angry about it?

6) Are there people in your home who are not scared of your fear?

7) Were they ever scared of it? When, and for how long?

8) Are there people in your home who get angry about the same thing?

9) What do they do to not be scared of it?

10) What do they do to not be angry about it?

11) Has anything bad happened to you regarding the fear?

12) How many days have you had the fear, but nothing bad has happened?

13) Has anything bad happened to you regarding your anger?

14) How many days have you had the anger, but nothing bad has happened?

Now that you have finished, read over all your data and see if you discovered any surprising information. Next, pick the most interesting or hopeful detail you'd like to remember and write it below.

Your Positive Discovery: ____

____

Let's go back to Phoebe's test-taking fear and use it as an example. Pheobe discovered that she did very well on 90% of her tests. So instead of thinking about a possible bad outcome before a test, instead she focused on her positive discovery and used it to calm her fear and anxiety surrounding test-taking.

Now I want you to focus on *your* positive discovery—I mean really think about it. Keep it in your thoughts for about 20–30 seconds. Have a parent help you keep track of time. I want you to do this each day you are working on your fears. You can even write down (or draw) your positive discovery on sticky notes and place them around your living space. These reminders will help you take in positive thoughts even when you are doing other things. Lastly, remember I said I would tell you more about positive thoughts? Here it is:

> With a little effort you can teach your brain to notice positive things just as easily as it remembers scary ones. A few seconds of positive thoughts, practiced daily, is all it takes to activate the brain and strengthen its ability to hold onto positive information as well as it holds onto negative information.* Pretty cool right?

* HORNET TALK

"Recent research shows that spending time focusing on positive thoughts helps the brain remember positive details as well as it remembers dangerous ones. When we do this daily, we build our positive memory bank, and we tend to feel happier."

Activity: New, Nice, and Natural

Now that you know just how helpful it is to focus on positive details, we're going to learn about an activity that will help you gather positive information and put it to work for you. Making a daily practice of taking in positive details is fun, and can actually start to balance your hornet's nest and help you feel less fearful and less angry. I call it, *The Three N's,* or *New, Nice, and Natural*. First you will learn about this activity, and at the end of this section, I have included a worksheet for you to practice on.

Something New

Your first task is to find something *new*—something you either haven't noticed before, or haven't focused on very closely. For example, maybe you have walked past a number of bookshelves in your school library and haven't really looked at what is on those shelves. Maybe you have eaten bananas many times, but you haven't really noticed all the colors in the skin, or how the banana tastes as you eat it. Or maybe you've lived in your house for years, but there are rooms you haven't spent much time in. Once you find something new, take 20 to 30 seconds and really focus on it.

Something Nice

Second, you get to notice something *nice.* Here too there are many possibilities—something nice someone says about you, or something nice you share with someone else. It could be your day going as planned, or a change in plans that turned out better than you expected. Perhaps Mom made your favorite dinner; or maybe you found your favorite pajamas clean and warm, ready to put on just before bed. Whatever the nice thing happens to be, make sure to give it a smile, and hold onto its memory for 20 to 30 seconds.

Something Natural

And third, find something *natural*. This last item is endless. You might notice spring grass poking through the melting snow of winter. You could watch the birds that live near your home and keep track of what they are busy doing. Or perhaps on your walk to school you pause to admire a tree that has been there for more years than you have been alive.

Why new, nice, and natural?

When we are engaged in new experiences, our brain uses areas that are specialized in gathering as much new information as they can. New stimulation is naturally more intriguing to us, and as a result we are able to pay attention longer. (For an example of this, think back to the first time you saw your favorite movie. Chances are even though you love rewatching it over and over, the movie doesn't quite give you the same excited feeling that you felt the first time you saw it.)

The practice of finding nice things helps balance out the brain's natural ability to remember negative things, giving it equal time to gather positive experiences. When we notice positive things we feel happier and less anxious.

And finally, when we focus on natural things it helps us to stay in the moment and avoid worrying about the past or the future. What is happening outdoors is happening right there at that very moment. And so when we focus on nature, or spend time in nature, we are able to reflect on that moment, too.

What are your three N's for today?

Something New, Something Nice, Something Natural

As you practice taking in the positive information around you, record your observations below. (You can use the back of this sheet if you need more room.)

. . . .

SOMETHING NEW

Find something in your environment that you haven't noticed before or given much attention to. Take a few seconds and really focus on it.

SOMETHING NICE

Remember one nice thing that someone said about you or that happened to you today. Hold onto this memory for 20 to 30 seconds.

SOMETHING NATURAL

Take a moment to observe something from nature, such as the clouds, a tree, or the birds that live around your home.

CHAPTER 5

What If Something Scary and Dangerous Really Did Happen?

Some of you may have lived through something really scary that started your worrying. Because you were so frightened, you may need to spend some extra time to work on that memory.

The goal for you is to tell the whole story of what happened. You can write the story down, or record your story on an audio device. Try to remember as many details as you can, just like we did in the fear-free memory—the time of year, who was involved, what happened afterward, and any other details you can remember. Then I want you to practice telling the story a number of times. Be sure to tell the story to a person you trust.

You may feel scared the first few times you try to do this. As you get better and better at telling the story, you'll notice that your body doesn't get as scared as you recount what happened. This is because with each retelling, the brain starts to shift what it remembers—and it may focus on different details. Eventually, the more you tell the story, your brain will remember the event without as many of the physical sensations of fear; and it will move this negative memory out of its fear file into its history file. Once there, you won't be as scared. In fact, you might even start to focus on positive details, like how you managed to survive, or something else you learned about yourself. Finding these positive details helps us grow stronger, and better able to handle new challenges. Is that cool or what?

NOTE TO PARENTS: If doing this step alone is just too scary for you or your child, you might benefit from seeing your very own therapist to help you through this process. If you (the listener) get too emotional hearing your child's story, your child might become even more scared. Then it will be harder to change how your child responds to the memory. A therapist is trained to sit with you and your child and help you both work towards feeling less afraid and upset. Sharing fearful or traumatic events with someone you trust is one kind of activity that helps. But there are other ways to help too, and this is where a mental health worker can really help you find the right approach.

CHAPTER SIX

Using Your Hippo-Brain

Throughout this workbook we have talked a lot about your hornet-brain. Now it's time to learn about your hippo-brain.

Let's go back to your imagination. Remember the drawing you made of your hornet and hippo on the *What's in Your Head?* worksheet on page 11? Believe it or not, you have been using your hippo-brain during some of the activities so far, and you didn't even know you were using it. Now you will learn how this works.

So, turn on your amazing imagination again—but this time I want you to pretend that you are a hippo. You live in Africa with your friend hornet; but you don't live in a hive. Your home is a grassy savannah near a slow-moving river. Trees line the riverbanks, offering shade from the hot, African sun. You are very big and solid on your feet. You are stable and very balanced. As your skin soaks up the sun's rays, you notice that you feel hot, so you walk to the trees at the edge of the water. You step in. It feels refreshing on your legs—so much so that you go further in, up to your knees. A few more steps and the water level reaches your belly. You continue. Now you are in up to your shoulders. Finally you are almost entirely under water, with just the top of your head and the tip of your nose breaking the water's surface. You feel solid and safe deep in the current. You are relaxed. With your body at rest and supported by the cool water, you are ready to use your senses and take in all that you hear, feel, taste, smell, and see. You are now an information-gathering machine.

You take a big, deep breath in through your nose, recognizing the familiar, muddy scent of the water. Slowly, you let that big breath out through your nose. You gaze out over the water. You observe its many colors—lighter in places where the sun hits, and darker in the shade. Again, you take another big, deep breath through your nose. You watch the delicate bugs that are hopping across the water's silky surface. Ripples nearby indicate that something is moving in the water with you. You slowly exhale, and take another big, deep breath. You have been in this river many times. In fact, you grew up in this river, and usually the ripples are caused by the little fish that live in the river with you. What do you think is moving the water? What are you imagining? *Write it below*.

———————————————————————————

———————————————————————————

———————————————————————————

If you are still pretending that you are a hippo who knows all about your river home, you might have imagined that the ripples were caused by some little fish, nibbling at your legs. Because hippo-you has felt this so many times before, you might think, *Oh, it is normal for fish to be in the water, too.*

This thought is not scary, so you stay calm and relaxed, and even appreciate the ticklish feeling as the fish gently nibble on your thick, hippo skin. However, if you thought that something else was in the water with you—something scary, like an alligator—maybe you were using your hornet-brain, and you might have felt afraid.

Let's try using your hippo imagination again. Time has passed. You have been in the water for awhile now, and you have been watching a beautiful bird near a nest in one of the trees on the river's edge. You've been enjoying his cheerful song. You watch him leave the tree, and a few moments later you feel something land on your head. What is your thought about that? Are you thinking about it from the hippo's perspective? *Write it below*.

———————————————————————————

———————————————————————————

———————————————————————————

What could it be? If you were thinking like a hippo, you would guess that the bird you were watching a few moments before had just landed on your head. Would the hippo be scared? If you guessed no, you are right! Hippos don't mind birds on their heads, because birds often come to visit looking for tasty bugs on the hippo's skin. So, if you thought the bird was there to be friendly, you would not be scared at all. In fact, you might be happy that the bird is being so helpful.

Now, if the hippo had never had a bird on her head before, she might not know what to think. Fear could be her response, or even anger—I mean no one gave that bird permission to land on her head! But in these examples, the hippo calmly used information she had gathered about her environment, and did not jump to a negative conclusion.

Just like hippos do, when we use our hippo-brain we slow down our reactions and look for more information about what is happening in our environment before we decide if we need to be scared or angry. In other words, we pause to gather information, and then we decide what needs to be done. When the brain is in hippo-mode* it is not scared, it is *curious-and-in-control*.

* HIPPO TALK

"The main area in the brain being used when in 'hippo-mode' is called the **hippocampus**. The hippocampus takes in the context of a situation and moves information to our long-term memory. When we use our hippocampus, activity in the amygdala (hornet) slows down, leaving us feeling much less scared or angry, and better able to learn and respond to the environment around us."

Pause and Find the Hippocampus

Now that we know what our hippo brain is called, go back to the *Color Your Brain* worksheet on page 15 and pinpoint where the hippocampus is inside the brain. If you haven't done so, see if you can color in the hippocampus. I will pause for a moment while you find it...

Okay what did you think? Where was it? How close was it to the hornet (amygdala)? Pretty close, right? In fact they sit right next to each other and even have a relationship to each other.

When your hornet is busy buzzing around in fight-or-flight mode, the hippo gets quiet and can have a hard time being curious-and-in-control. But when the hippo is running, the hornet settles down, too. They are both there for you to use when you need them.

CHAPTER SEVEN

Your Hippo Brain Comes to the Rescue

Let's go back to Africa, to the river where the hippo has been spending her day. Just like the hippo does, let's take a few, deep breaths through our nose, which slowly fills up our lungs, and then slowly let the air out.

Now, let's imagine that the hippo just heard the same lioness that the hornet heard in chapter two. The hippo's brain goes into curious-and-in-control mode, and maybe she even takes a few more deep breaths. She watches the lioness approach the river, and takes a moment to calculate how far the lioness is from her location. It turns out the lioness is pretty far away.

Taking in another deep breath, she considers what she knows about lions. She knows that running away from one isn't always the best strategy. In fact, sometimes running from a predator can draw attention to you and make you the target. In many situations, remaining calm keeps you safe.

She glances at the other hippos nearby. They look calm and remain still. Lastly she observes that the lioness has stopped underneath a nearby tree where her two cubs are playing in the bushes. When they finish with their game the lioness and her cubs get to their feet, and slowly wander away.

As it turned out, the hippo was not in any danger after all. Her curiosity helped her gather needed information (where the lioness was going); and the feeling of being in control helped her stay calm, and use the information she already had (her knowledge of predators) to make an informed decision before she reacted.

That was a tremendous amount of information gathered while in hippo-mode! Can you see how helpful this is for informing yourself about a situation? If you had been using your hornet-brain, you might have panicked and felt a lot of fear and anxiety even though (in this example) the danger passed quickly. Or you might have felt threatened because the lioness was near your pond, and your fear made you angry. Also, you might not have gathered anywhere near this much information.

Hippo-mode lets you use the information you already have to gather the information that you really need to learn from and make decisions in the moment. And guess what? It takes practice to do this. So the goal (if you choose to accept it!) is to keep practicing this skill until you feel really good at it. When you are in hippo-mode, you feel calm and confident, and the more often you are able to go into hippo-mode, the easier it gets.

Scientists say, "what fires together, wires together,"* which means that the neurons in the brain get stronger and stronger as you repeat a behavior or thought pattern. So the more you practice, the stronger your brain grows.

I bet if you practice gathering information and putting that information in your memory banks, you will feel really good about your ability to be calm, stay curious, and feel in control. Or, to think about it in hornet and hippo terms—keep your hippo pond full of information, while keeping the hornet's nest nice and small.

* HIPPO TALK

"What fires together, wires together is a common description that scientists use to describe the brain's ability to strengthen neuronal connections."

Gathering Information Like a Hippo, and Your Hippo Pond

Now that you know how helpful it is to gather information with your hippo-brain, I want you to give it a try with something you have an interest in. You can pick anything you want. If you're unsure where to start, you might be inspired by the suggestions that I have included for you below:

- Interview a friend or family member to find out more about his or her life.

- Explore your home to discover how many different kinds of animals or plants you have in your environment.

- Gather information about a topic you'd like to know more about.

When you're done, notice how you feel. Did you learn something new? I bet you did.

Now, let's do a bit more. This time, let's get curious about *you*. I want you to fill a hippo pond with a few things you really like about yourself. For example, what are you interested in? Is there something special you've done, or something that you are proud of?

I'd also like you to pick three things you are grateful for. Do you remember my fear-free moment about my time on the beach in California? Well, I'm very grateful I had that experience. So, if I were doing this activity, I might like to include a description or a picture of that memory in my hippo pond.

On the next page you will find a hippo pond of your very own. Fill it with words or pictures of your interests, what you are proud of, and the things that you are grateful for. Keep your pond where you can see it and add to it any time you want. You can also make a copy of the worksheet for a family member, so they can fill their pond, too.

Your Hippo Pond

Fill this pond with words, drawings or pictures of your interests or things you are grateful for.

Mindful Moment 3:
Hippo

Find a comfortable spot either on a chair or the floor. Take a moment to notice how your body feels. Make any needed adjustments that you need to, until your body feels at peace. Notice your breath as it moves in and out. As you sit quietly, you might notice changes in how comfortable you feel. If at any time during this mindful practice you feel uncomfortable, adjust what you need to until you feel content.

On page 69 you will find a picture of a hippo drinking water on a riverbank in Africa. Take a few moments to study the illustration, which is full of many details. Use the details that you discover to tell a story about what the hippo is doing in the picture. Then, if you like, use your imagination to make the story your own. Maybe something happens in the story that you or the hippo are grateful for. You can even color the picture in if you like. Go ahead and begin now.

Now that you have your story about the hippo, use the worksheet on page 73 to write it down. Try to make the story you saw in your head come alive with your words.

When you are done, let a parent read the story to you while you sit back and listen. You can even close your eyes while you listen to your story, focusing on your breath as it moves in and out. After the story is over, keep resting in your mindful moment, noticing each breath you take. Pause for two minutes before ending this mindful moment.

Your Mindful Hippo Story

Write your hippo story in the space below. Try to include as many details as you can. There's more room to write on the back of this sheet if you need it.

CHAPTER EIGHT

Finding Your Balance

We are now going to work on balance. Not the physical kind of balance that you use on a balance beam. I'm referring to your emotional footing. With practice, you will be able to balance your brain between hornet-mode (survival mode), and hippo mode (curious-and-in-control mode).

In this chapter I want you to use your hippo brain to gather some important information. To start, think back to the last time you got noticeably scared or angry. Maybe it was just yesterday, or maybe it happened awhile ago. Rate on a scale of one to ten just how scared or angry you felt (10 = most scared; 1 = not scared at all). Were you able to give it a score?

How scared or angry were you?   __________

Next I want you to think back again to that moment of fear and decide just how dangerous the situation was. Use your hippo-brain and think about it again. Were you in danger, or did you just feel like you were? Use the same rating scale as above (10 = great danger; 1 = safe and sound).

How dangerous was it?   __________

Now let's examine your numbers. Was your scared or angry number bigger than the danger number? Chances are, if you are using this workbook, your first number will be bigger than the actual danger number. But now that you are going to be working on finding your balance, these numbers will grow closer and closer to each other. For this to happen you just need to keep track of your fear and anger responses, and your evaluation of how dangerous the situation was afterwards.

The goal of this activity is for you to start becoming aware of when your response and actual danger are different. If they are close to each other, congratulations! You are in balance. If they are far apart, the next few chapters will help you bring your scores closer together.

On the following page you will find a worksheet for you to start a log of these events. I call it *Finding Your Balance*.

Parents, feel free to make an extra copy for you, too. You might find there are moments when your parenting is more balanced than other moments. The more you are in balance, the easier it will be for your kids to find balance, too. They learn so much from us.

Finding Your Balance

On this page you can keep track of when you get scared, and how dangerous the situation really is. Rate your fear or worry on a scale of 1 to 10, where one is not scared at all, and 10 is the most scared you have ever been. Then notice if your numbers match. Are you in emotional balance, or are you still working on it?

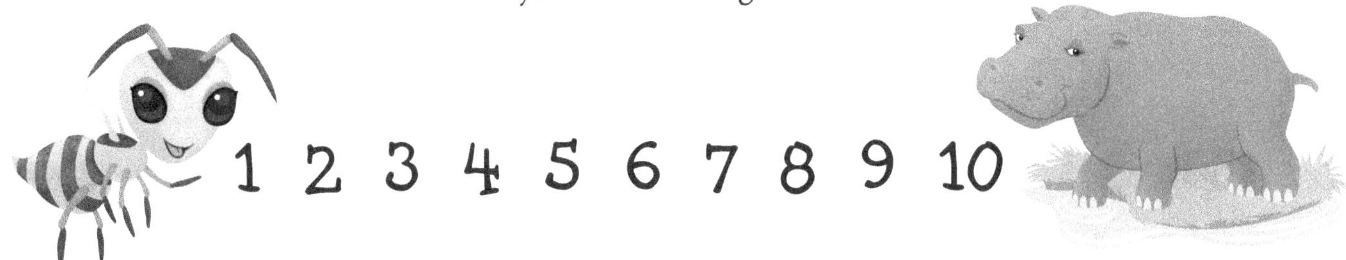

Describe your fear or worry:	How scared are you?	What happened? What rating would you give the event?	Balanced ... yes or no?
I'm afraid to take my test.	*8 out of 10*	*I got a B+, so it was a 2 out of 10.*	*Not yet.*

1)

2)

3)

4)

5)

I hope you enjoyed working on your balance worksheet. Be sure to keep coming back to it whenever you feel big emotions. The more aware you are, the easier it is to find balance. This is how mindfulness really works.

Pause and Find Your Prefrontal Cortex

Ready for another activity that can help you find balance? Let's go back to the *Color Your Brain* worksheet on page 15 again. This time, find the **prefrontal cortex**. Let's pause while you find it...

Okay, what did you think? Where was it? How close was it to the hornet (amygdala)? It was just behind your forehead, a little bit away from the hornet and hippo, right?

You use this part of your brain in decision-making. The prefrontal cortex takes in all of the information that has been gathered by the hippo and hornet, and then uses those details to make decisions. Additionally, this part of the brain will get stronger as you get older. In fact it takes 25 years (on average) for the prefrontal cortex to finish all of its development!

Every time you practice making a decision, you build strength in this part of your brain. Mindful moments also strengthen the prefrontal cortex. Slowing down your thoughts and watching where they go; or guiding them (as we have been doing in our mindful moments) helps us make clearer, less impulsive decisions. It helps us calm our reactions overall, and be more in the moment.

I haven't given the prefrontal cortex an animal name like I did for the amygdala (hornet) and hippocampus (hippo), because I was hoping you would come up with your own name for that part of your brain.

Think about an animal that feels like your guide. In other words, what type of animal would you use to represent you and your values, and the kind of decisions you make? For example, my animal guide is a sea otter, because I share the sea otter's playful spirit and love of water.

What animal can you see at the front of your brain? Pick one of your very own who will help lead your way. On page 81 you will find a space to draw or paste a picture of the animal you see in your prefrontal cortex. Then, any time you are working on things that are hard remember, your animal guide can help you move between hornet-mode and hippo-mode whenever you need to.

Your Animal Guide

Use the head illustration below to draw a picture or place a photo of the animal that represents your prefrontal cortex.

Mindful Moment 4:
On Top of a Mountain

Find a comfortable spot either on a chair or the floor. Take a moment to notice how your body feels. Make any needed adjustments until your body feels at peace. Focus on your breath as it moves in and out. As you sit quietly, you might observe changes in how comfortable you feel. If at any time during this mindful practice you feel uncomfortable, adjust what you need until you feel content.

Next find a point in the room to focus on. Or if you like, close your eyes and focus inside yourself. Have a parent or other adult read the mindful moment on the following page out loud. Your only job is to listen, breathe, and observe where your thoughts take you. You will be given a chance to sit quietly at the end.

Mindful Moment: Your Mountain

(Parent: Read slowly, pausing between each sentence.)

For this mindful practice I want you to imagine that you are a big, beautiful mountain. Perhaps you live along the ocean, and your slopes are covered with fields and giant trees. Or perhaps your snowy peak overlooks a small lake, which is fed by bubbling streams. Elk, deer or foxes might live with you. Maybe an eagle is flying high above. What other birds live here? Are there people on your mountain? Are there buildings? It's your mountain. You can put whatever you want on it. It might even have something that you are scared of, or something that you are grateful for. Sit quietly for a minute or two while you create your mountain. Notice your breath moving in and out.

Now that you have your mountain in your mind, you notice that one of the animals living at the base of your mountain sets off for the mountain's summit. You watch as it travels all the way to the top, passing all the details you created—trees, birds, buildings, bodies of water. If you included your fear or something you are grateful for on your mountain, the animal will walk past them, too. What does it see? I imagine it notices so many things along the way. When it reaches the top, I want you to switch your focus. Instead of the mountain, now pretend you are the animal. Look out as far as you can. How do you feel? Have you ever imagined anything so big? Take a minute to just sit and think about your mountain and how your body feels.

Use the next page to draw your mountain. Or search for a picture of the one you have in mind and paste it in the space provided. You can use this mindful practice whenever you feel scared. It is hard to feel scared for long if your fear is sitting on something as large and solid as your very own mountain.

Your Mountain

CHAPTER NINE

Curious-and-in-Control Strengthens the Whole Brain

There are many ways to strengthen your brain that will aid in reducing your fear and keep you feeling curious-and-in-control. I have broken these activities into four different types—breath, movement, activities for your brain, and body regulation. Some of them you will be familiar with if you have been practicing your M.E.D.S.—or if you have been finding your *Three N's* each day.

BREATHING ACTIVITIES

Concentrating on your breath helps you and your body feel calm and can help you get into curious-and-in-control mode rather than fight-or-flight mode. Breathing is something you don't usually think about. It is run by a part of your body called the **autonomic nervous system**. In other words, your breath is automatic! But when you take control of your breath and really notice how it feels, you are able to feel calm and in the moment. Many exercise classes like yoga teach breathing techniques, but you can practice them at home, too. Here are some activities to get you started.

1) Listen to Your Breath

(5 minute exercise using your breath and concentration)

Close your eyes and listen to your breath. Notice the sound it makes as it moves in and out of your nose or mouth. Decide if you are using your nose or mouth and stick with it. Listen to the different sounds you hear in-between each breath. Listen for the silence. Keep listening. Sometimes listening is hard, and your mind will wander to other things. If your thoughts wander, don't worry. Acknowledge that it happened, and then refocus on your breathing. If this is difficult, have a family member sit with you. Every 30 seconds have them remind you to keep listening to your breath. Each time your mind wanders and refocuses on your breathing you strengthen your hippo-brain.

2) Exhale Your Breath

(1–2 minute exercise using your breath)

To begin this conscious breathing exerise, I would like you to slow down your breath. First, empty your lungs by letting all the air out. Next, slowly inhale as you (or your parent) count to five. Once your lungs are full, exhale as slowly as you can. See if you can make your exhale longer than your inhale by a few seconds. Keep repeating this conscious breathing for a few minutes; five seconds in, seven seconds out. If your mind or your breath wander, that's okay. Just come back to it.

3) Breathe like a Hippo

(5 minute exercise using breath and imagination)

Close your eyes and take a deep breath through your nose. Imagine you are a hippo resting in a cool pond with only your shoulders, head, and nose above the surface. Breathe slowly through your nose. As you do, use your imagination to feel the water around you. Notice what is on the surface. Now notice what's near the edge of the pond. With each breath, extend the exhale as long as you can and imagine your breath rippling out across the water's surface.

4) How Strong Are Your Lungs?

(1–2 minutes using your breath and body awareness)

Did you know your lungs are so strong, you can move your whole body while breathing? To begin this body awareness activity, lie down on the floor with your tummy on the ground. Take a very big breath. Do you feel how your powerful lungs lift your body up? Now that your lungs are full, slowly exhale. Pay attention to how your body feels as it slowly returns to the ground. Next, I want you to roll over onto your back. Bend your knees with your feet on the floor and your knees touching. Place a small object (or your hands) on your chest. Continue to take more big breaths, but this time watch the object on your chest move up and down.

5) Big Bad Wolf Breath

(1–2 minutes using breath and imagination)

Pretend you are the Big Bad Wolf and use your powerful breath to blow something down. It could be some toys, or even an imaginary house. It's your imagination, so you get to decide.

6) Buddy Breathing

(2–4 minutes using breath, touch, and eye contact)

For this breathing exercise you will need to face someone. Reach out your right hands. Interlock your fingers with theirs, and put your thumbs together, like you are going to thumb wrestle. Next, one of you will lead by moving your thumb to the right while taking in a big breath. Then, move your thumb to the left and slowy exhale. The partner will follow the lead of the other. After a few rounds of this, you can swich so the other person can be the leader. The touch and eye contact, along with the slow exhales, will help calm the body.

MOVEMENT ACTIVITIES

We all know that exercise is good for our overall health. But exercise is also an important tool we can use not only to strengthen our heart; but to calm it down as well, which can often help to minimize a number of fear symptoms. In addition to being good for the body, exercise also promotes brain health by helping the brain work more efficiently. A more efficient brain means that you will be better able to gather and remember new information. These skills are important when you use your hippo-brain.

1) Exercise of Any Kind

(20–30 minutes a day)

What kind of exercise do you like? How often do you do it? Exercise gets the heart rate up and gives the brain energy after you are done. Exercise helps us learn better, and it also helps us keep on track with our goals. If you want to make any kind of change, exercise will help you reach your goal. The most important thing to keep in mind when you choose your exercise is that you pick something you love. If you love to do it, you will keep it up. Aim for at least 20–30 minutes a day—but start where you can. Even five minutes of exercise when you feel anxious can help calm your body. (Parents, if your child already has physical education built into their day through school or extracurricular activities, you may not need to add more on that day. If your school offers intensive summer physical education vs. daily exercise, it is more helpful to the body and learning to keep exercise in a daily routine.)

2) Chop Down Your Hornet's Nest

(1-2 minutes using body, breath, and imagination)

For this exercise, I'd like you imagine the hornet's nest of negative experiences that your hornet has been building in your brain. It's time to get rid of it, keeping only what you need. We are going to use your body and your imagination to chop it down. To begin, stand tall and put your hands together, interlacing your fingers. Next, take your index fingers and straighten them to make an imaginary chopper. Now that you have your chopper, raise it way above your head while filling your lungs with air. If you can, pull the air in through your nose. When you are ready, swiftly bring your chopper and your arms down to the ground while you blow the air out your mouth. You can also make a noise when you exhale. Repeat this exercise as many times as you need to chop down your nest (at least 3–6 times).

3) **Squat Spot**

(1–2 minute exercise using your body)

When we squat, pressure is placed on the vagus nerve and slows out heart rate. Whenever you feel scared, this movement will help your body return to a state of calm. To begin, squat down and put your arms around your knees. If you are comfortable, stay there for a few minutes. When you are finished, slowly stand up or sit in a chair to avoid feeling light-headed. If you can't squat, bend at the waist and rest your hands on your knees—as much as your body will allow. This exercise can even be done while seated in a chair. With your feet resting on the floor, lower your torso onto your lap.

4) **Lie Down, Hands Up**

(1–2 minutes using body and breath)

Lie down on the floor with a pillow propped under your knees. If it makes you more comfortable you can also put a small pillow under your head. Next, raise your arms over your head and hold your hands together. Take a few deep breaths and notice how open your lungs feel. If you were experiencing any stomach pain before this exercise began (from an anxious tummy, for example), you might notice it fade away. Remain in this position as long as you feel comfortable. You can also do this exercise while you are getting ready to fall asleep.

5) **Monkey Arms**

(1–2 minute exercise using your body)

This movement will not only give you a boost of energy when

you need it; but when you are finished, it will help you pay attention to your next activity. To begin, stand with your arms at your sides and your feet shoulder-width apart. From your waist, twist from side to side. As you move, you will notice that your arms will naturally swing. Let them. As they do, tap your hip before you twist to the other side. Keep swinging and tapping for a minute or more.

6) Balance Like a Tree

(5–10 minute exercise using your body)

For this movement, stand with your feet firmly on the ground and imagine you are a tall tree with roots that go down into the earth. Once you feel solid and stable, lift your left foot and place it just below your right knee; or, if you are more flexible, you can place it above the knee—just be careful not place it directly on your knee, which could cause injury. Once you feel balanced, lift your hands up over your head, reaching for the sky. If you can, try to add some wind in your "branches" and sway lightly back and forth, keeping a steady, balanced movement. After a minute or so, return your foot to the ground and repeat with the other side.

BRAIN ACTIVITIES

Keeping your brain healthy and flexible will help prepare you for all the new experiences that life brings. The following activities are great tools that you can use to increase your attention span, and to recall and focus on positive details, which will help keep your hornet's nest (negativity bias) from taking over.

1) Something New, Something Nice, and Something Natural or "The Three N's"

(5–10 minutes using your brain)

This brain exercise will not only help you strengthen your information gathering skills (hippo-brain), but it may also help you feel calmer in an envrionment where you usually get anxious. If you need a reminder about what the Three N's are, see page 48. The worksheet for this activity can be found on page 51.

2) Find Your Calm

(mindful awareness throughout the day)

In this activity, you will use a notebook or a calendar to focus on moments when you are calm and anxiety free. If you experience fear throughout the day, I want you to notice how many hours (or minutes) the fear is absent. Keep track of these fear-free moments in your notebook or calendar. When you have managed five days with no fear, reward yourself with special time with your parents, other special family members, or friends. The best rewards are those that keep family relationships strong.

3) Art Time

(10–30 minutes using your brain and imagination)

A great sense of calm comes over us when we let ourselves dive into an art project. The materials you choose are up to you, as long as there is no specific outcome you need. In other words, it is the act of doing art that is calming, not the finished project. So if you want to draw, be sure to let your mind wander and have fun. Don't get caught up in perfection. Just enjoy how it feels.

4) Build Your Own Sandbox

(10–30 minutes using your brain, body sensations, and imagination)

You can assemble a simple sandbox where you can make "sandpictures." All you need is a plastic container with a lid and play sand. (You can find plastic containers of all different kinds in most home stores, and play sand can be found at stores where they sell wood or garden supplies.) Choose a container that is at least 2 to 3 feet long, and at least 1½ feet wide. Fill the box about halfway. Select small toys, rocks or other items from nature, and then away you go! Put together any picture you want. There is no right or wrong picture, and you don't have to keep it; so it's a nice way to spend time processing ideas without planning for a particular outcome. Let your mind wander.

5) **Something I Am Grateful For**

(2–3 minutes each day)

There are many things that happen to us that we are grateful for. Take a moment each day to share with someone one thing that you are grateful for. When you take time for this activity, just like when you look for "The Three N's," you help your brain gather—and remember—the good emotions that you feel every day.

6) **Mindful Moments**

Remember the mindful moments that we learned about in this workbook? Choose the ones you like and practice these whenever you want. A daily practice of mindful moments will keep your decision-making strong and help you get into hippo-mode more easily. The ones we have done are:

Your Body Is Looking Out for You (pg. 27), *Fear-Free/Anger-Free Moment* (pg. 35), and *On Top of a Mountain* (pg. 83).

BODY REGULATION

There are a few things that we all need to do to survive and thrive, like eat, drink water, and sleep (and breathe, but we already covered that). But sometimes when we are anxious, sleep and hunger are affected in a negative way. If you are having trouble with sleep or appetite, decide which one you want to work on first. If you can, try to work on both. If you do, you will have much more energy to handle any challenge of the day. Here are some more details to consider.

1) **Drink Water**

When you are taking in fluids your body responds like there is no danger present. Keep a water bottle nearby and sip throughout the day. Parents, many schools will now let your child have a water bottle at his or her desk, so be sure to ask to let your child do this.

2) **Don't Forget to Eat Just the Right Amount**

If you get anxious a lot, sometimes you don't feel like eating, or you feel like eating all the time. Hunger can feel like anxiety, so it's helpful to keep healthy snacks with you; that way, if you do feel hungry, you can put a little something in your belly. Snacks like veggies, or those with proteins and healthy fats digest more slowly and are better for managing anxiety than carbohydrates or sugar snacks. If you have any questions regarding the amount of food or the best kinds for you, it would be best to consult your pediatrician or a nutritionist. Changes in your diet for the better can greatly improve your tolerance for stress and anxiety.

3) **Good Night Sleep**

Sleep is the body's way of getting itself ready for the challenges of the day. While you are sleeping, your brain is busy filing away all the things you have learned and experienced. If you can't get the sleep you need at night, you might start to feel more stressed during the day. So make sure you are getting enough (see Sleep Chart on page 121). Parents, varying children's sleep schedules can be more disruptive for them than it is for an adult, so try to keep them on a routine, even when they are not in school. This regularity can really make a difference in managing anxiety. If you are not sure if your child is getting enough sleep, try adding an extra hour to see if it makes a difference.

4) **Turn Off Your Buzzing Mind**

• Drain the Brain

Sometimes it's hard to turn off the thoughts of the day. You might replay something that happened that upset you, or go over a list of things you want to do the next day. Or maybe your imagination keeps wandering. When this happens it can be hard to fall asleep. Sometimes, putting these thoughts down on paper helps drain the brain so that you can go to sleep. Keep a notebook by your bed, and use it to write down these running thoughts that are preventing you from sleeping. If writing is hard for you, have a parent help.

• Simple Stretch

Another trick to calming your mind before sleep is to perform a simple stretch while in bed. To begin, sit up from your pillow with your legs stretched out before you. Now, gently lower your torso and reach for your toes. See if you can relax in this position for a minute or two. You might notice some tightness in your back and lower legs fade away. When you lie back down, notice how much calmer you feel. Now you are ready to turn your mind off and sleep.

WEEKLY PRACTICE

Choosing Your Activities

There are a lot of activities to choose from. Hopefully some of them sound interesting to you. Please start by selecting one from each type and work on them for one week. There are enough activities for you to use for at least four weeks. At the end of the four weeks choose your favorites and keep doing them for as long as they are helpful.

BREATHING ACTIVITIES

Listen to Your Breath
Exhale Your Breath
Breathe Like a Hippo
How Strong Are Your Lungs
Big Bad Wolf Breath
Buddy Breathing

BRAIN ACTIVITIES

The Three N's
Find Your Calm
Art Time
Build Your Own Sandbox
Something I Am Grateful For
Mindful Moments

MOVEMENT ACTIVITIES

Exercise of Any Kind
Chop Down Your Hornet's Nest
Squat Spot
Lie Down, Hands Up
Monkey Arms
Balance Like a Tree

BODY REGULATION

Drink Water
Don't Forget to Eat
Good Night Sleep
Turn Off Your Buzzing Mind

Weekly Practice

Write down the activities you have chosen
to work on each week in the space provided below.

Week One:

BREATHING ACTIVITY _______________________________

MOVEMENT ACTIVITY _______________________________

BRAIN ACTIVITY _______________________________

BODY REGULATION _______________________________

Week Two:

BREATHING ACTIVITY _______________________________

MOVEMENT ACTIVITY _______________________________

BRAIN ACTIVITY _______________________________

BODY REGULATION _______________________________

Week Three:

BREATHING ACTIVITY _______________________________

MOVEMENT ACTIVITY _______________________________

BRAIN ACTIVITY _______________________________

BODY REGULATION _______________________________

Week Four:

BREATHING ACTIVITY   _________________________________

MOVEMENT ACTIVITY   _________________________________

BRAIN ACTIVITY   _________________________________

BODY REGULATION   _________________________________

List Your Favorites:

BREATHING ACTIVITY   _________________________________

MOVEMENT ACTIVITY   _________________________________

BRAIN ACTIVITY   _________________________________

BODY REGULATION   _________________________________

Keep It Up!

Daily practice will make the biggest difference, even if it is only for a few minutes a day. If you can do more—say 10 to 12 minutes a day—that's even better!

CHAPTER TEN

Planting S.E.E.D.'s

Parenting with the Hornet and Hipppo in Mind: Fear, Anger, Curiosity and Connection in the Family Culture

We now know that fear and anger are normal, and that they serve an important purpose in our survival. We also know that too much focus on fearful or angry reactions limits the brain's ability to pay attention, and to maintain healthy feelings of curiosity and control.

What you may not know is that people pass emotional information on to each other even when they don't know that they are doing it. This is because we develop in relation to others and we are social learners. Family culture, as well as connections with those in your family, directly affect how the brain grows. Children are wired to connect to others, and they start watching what others are doing from the day they are born. The fact that children are watching us turns out to be one of their most powerful learning tools.

For example, one of the earliest examples of social learning happened when your child was only a few weeks old. Your child had been watching you smiling at him for those first few weeks, and then—*BOOM!* He smiled right back. Most parents remember this powerful moment of intense, emotional connection. The connection between you both continues to intensify as your child develops more and more physical and cognitive skills.

The fact that your child is watching you also turns out to be one of your most powerful parenting tools. Not only do they watch you, they try to copy you as well. I bet you even have some examples of this. Maybe you remember them parroting something that you said—such as a bad word, a unique phrase, or expressing one of your points of view. Or perhaps you remember a time when they tried to do something for you that you had done for them—singing a lullaby to help you sleep, for example. Or perhaps they tried to take your temperature when you were sick, the way you always do for them.

One of my favorite examples of social learning takes place in parks everywhere. Maybe you remember this happening to you:

> You and your child take a trip to the park. As she dashes over to the giant jungle gym, you find a nice spot on a bench where you believe you can watch over her. Busy and happy, your child uses her big arms and legs to pull her whole body up onto the jungle gym, when suddenly she loses her grip and tumbles to the ground.

What happens next depends on how hurt she is, and what you, as the parent, do. Most kids will immediately look for their parent after they fall to see what their parent tells them. This interaction is called **social learning**, or **social referencing**.

If you maintain a calm expression, your child will only cry if she is in pain or needs help. However, if you panic and show that panic on your face; or if you rush over to your child with fear or anger; then your child is likely to feel panic *in addition* to any hurt they felt from the fall. This is one way we pass emotions on to each other. We get scared, and then they get scared.

There are many positive emotions we pass to our children, too. Children light up when we get excited about one of their accomplishments. Of course the accomplishment alone helps them feel good about themselves—but it feels even better when we get excited with them. Hopefully most of the emotions shared between you and your child are positive ones. But when helping children balance fear with curiosity, it is important to take an inventory of your own level of fear and curiosity in the home. The more aware you are of when you are fearful, the better able you are to guide your child to a calm place.

This of course, takes being connected to your own emotions, which can be challenging. If you run more fearful, then your children will tend to be more fearful too, because children are particularly good social learners. This is what they are designed to do. But before you start worrying even more, remember the goal is not to eliminate all fears but to balance your reaction to the situation at hand.

Another example worth sharing is one that I experienced as a preschool teacher, in a class of twelve 2-year-olds. One day, one of the children came to class and became very angry after his mom left. He spent the first few minutes not wanting to talk to the other children or the teachers; and then he took his little hand and made a fist. As he moved his fist up and down he stomped his foot and said, "Gosh darn it!"

Well, actually I am editing the exact words that he used—but you get the idea. He sounded like an angry adult, and he was imitating something he had most likely heard one (or both) of his parents say.

This reaction showed me that he was doing two important things. First, he was letting me know that he was angry. Secondly, he was giving me an opportunity to talk to him about how he was feeling. In other words, he was giving me an opportunity to try to connect with him and his brain, which was sending angry feelings throughout his body. If I had taken his heart rate, I am sure it would have been elevated; and just as likely, his breathing would have been short and restricted. Angry and fearful, he wasn't taking in the caregivers around him. His arms and legs, energized with increased blood flow, were ready to run, or fight—evident by his stomping foot and clenched fist. Sound familiar?

It would have been easy to focus on the inappropriateness of his language. However, if I had done so, I would have missed two major skills this child was showing me—his ability to watch and copy others, and his ability to express emotion. These are skills children need.

So what can we do when a child gets angry and uses harsh words? Or what if a child is upset and tries to harm a sibling or even themselves? Those are situations we can't ignore.

To help you parent with the hornet and hippo in mind, I've put together a four-step guide that parents can use to help in these situations—I call it S.E.E.D.'s, and it stands for: <u>S</u>elf Calm, <u>E</u>mpathy for Emotion, <u>E</u>motions to the Body, and <u>D</u>irect with Respect. Over the next few pages I will describe each of the steps in detail, and at the end of this section you will find a handy card that you can cut out and keep with you to use whenever the need arises.

Step One: SELF CALM

Before we can really help our children, we need to look at how any angry or fearful situations make us—as parents—feel. If our fear or anger shoots up too, which it is likely to do, it's important to step back and calm our own emotional storm. The same **M.E.D.S.*** (movement, exhale breath, drink water, and squat spot) that we learned about on page 23, also work for parents—if you can give yourself a moment to step back from the situation.

One simple way to do this is to take a moment to check your heart rate and wait until it is back down to your normal resting beat. Taking this step will put you back in a more in-control feeling and better assist you in bridging back to your child and connecting to them.

Remember, if we approach them with our own strong emotions, whether it is anger, fear, or a combination of both, they will be less able to connect to us and take our guidance, and their emotions get bigger.

* HIPPO TALK

"Parents, you can use M.E.D.S. as well. If your kids are too distraught to join in, just let them watch you. Your self-calm will help them find theirs."

Step Two: EMPATHY TOWARDS EMOTIONS

Now that you're calm, the next step is to understand how your child feels. If they can describe their emotions, you can reflect them back using empathy*. The ability to empathize with others is one of our most powerful tools. When we're upset and we know someone understands how we feel, we calm down much more quickly.

For an example of this, let's look back at my preschooler whose mom left before he was ready. If you remember, he had just used adult language and made a fist to tell me how angry he was. My next step was to allow his emotion and try to empathize with it. To do this, I used an empathetic statement such as, "So it sounds like you felt angry when you noticed your mom was gone." If I was on the right track, he would calm down. Even if my guess was off the mark he might settle down and relax anyway, because I was trying to connect with him.

So when your child gets upset, lead with empathy, and try to let them know you understand *how* they feel well before you try to change *what* they feel. Parents often jump in and try to fix it too soon, which often seems like the parent is saying, "Don't feel that." In fact, telling your child not to feel that way may upset them even more. So keep it simple. Mirror what they tell you, and pause there, experiencing it a bit, too.

*** HIPPO TALK**

"Empathy is being in the mud pond with your child, not trying to clean the mud off."

Step Three: EMOTIONS TO THE BODY

Now that you've empathized with your child, the next step is to try and connect your child's emotions to any physical sensations happening in their body. For example you could say something like, "It looks like you could feel that anger in your arms and legs as you were stomping and making a fist."

If there isn't an obvious behavior, ask them where they feel the emotion in their body. They might say something like, "When I get angry, I can feel my heart beat."

Armed with this information, you can now help your child recognize the physical way in which their emotions are expressed by their body.*

In the example with my preschooler, I had him give me a few more stomps and shake his fist a few more times, knowing that the physical motions would help him release some of that fight-or-flight energy he was using. Finally, I asked him how he learned to stomp his foot and make that fist. This sort of detailed questioning helped him move to hippo-mode from hornet-mode, and reassured him that not only was it okay to talk about his experiences, but that I really noticed what he was doing in that moment.

* HIPPO TALK

"Noticing where you experience emotions in your body will give you meaningful information about where your hornet-brain connects to stress, and where you can focus to help let that stress go."

Step Four: DIRECT WITH RESPECT

The final step in S.E.E.D. parenting is to direct (or redirect) with respect. Now that you have practiced self calm with your M.E.D.S.; were able to use empathy to connect with your child's emotions; and helped connect those emotions to your child's body; you are now ready to direct your child in whatever way the situation requires. Due to your mutual calm, the exchange is more likely to be respectful, which feels better to you both.

Let's return one last time to my preschooler. Within a few minutes he felt better and was encouraged (or directed) to look around at the other children. He became curious about the class, and got back to the business of learning and playing. If he had said, "no," more empathy might have been needed before redirecting. After a little nudge to see if he was ready (and because he was feeling connected to his teacher), he became interested in the other children and was able to reconnect with his natural curiosity.*

If this had been you and your child, your mutual connection would enable your child to hear what you had to offer as a parent. As a result, you'd feel more capable of helping your child. Parenting is a difficult job, and we're not always going to do things just right. With the practice of self calm and empathy as our first two steps, steps three and four are also possible to achieve.

* HIPPO TALK

"After your child has started to calm down, he or she is much more ready to listen to what guidance you might have to offer—even it is just a hug or kiss."

So let's summarize these steps to parenting with the hornet and hippo in mind:

1. SELF CALM:

First, notice your own fear and anger, and then find a way to
gather your calm.

2. EMPATHY FOR EMOTIONS:

Allow your child's emotions to be expressed and try to
empathize.

3. EMOTIONS TO THE BODY:

Help them connect their emotions to what their body feels.

4. DIRECT WITH RESPECT:

Notice how connected they feel to you. When they feel connected
they are better able to hear your words, take in your guidance,
and respect what you have to offer them.

On the next page you will find a handy little shorthand you can copy onto a
3x5 card, or cut out to use as a reminder of the steps to parenting with the
hornet and hippo in mind.

S.E.E.D.'s

<u>S</u>ELF CALM

<u>E</u>MPATHY FOR EMOTION

<u>E</u>MOTIONS TO THE BODY

<u>D</u>IRECT WITH RESPECT

IN CONCLUSION

Parents, we have a huge opportunity to help our children not only by using what we have learned so far about our brains, but when we use ourselves as a guide.

If we leave a lot of fear and anger in the family environment, our kids will pick up on it. They will even use the same words we use to describe fearful or angry situations. Children pick up on these social cues as early as they are able to make eye contact, talk, and explore. Lots of fear in an environment can even start to feel normal to them, making it even harder for them to separate real danger from danger that is exaggerated.

The goal for parents is not to eliminate all things scary, but to build a family environment with structure, safety, and room to learn to explore the world without constant fear of harm. You can plant the S.E.E.D.'s of self calm, empathize with their emotions, and help them understand how emotions connect to the body. If you can do this, your directions will be heard and respected much more often than not.

Even if you just set out to notice your own emotional response, you will be better able to make changes in the directions that are best for you and your child.

So your challenge (if you choose to accept it!) is to become more mindful of yourself, and you will soon see your children do the same. If I plant the seed to start with just a breath, I know you will find the resources to plant your own S.E.E.D.'s.

HORNET'S NEST OR HIPPO POND

If you have read this far, you've already begun to look at fear and curiosity differently and are on the path to helping your child use his or her brain power to the fullest. After finding your own calm, I would encourage you to start tuning in to what kind of information your family focuses on. Are you building a hornet's nest or a hippo pond?

For example, do you watch the daily news or listen to news on the radio or internet with your child in the room? If so, check in with your child to see if this is something that leaves them feeling scared. As we grow older, we learn to make decisions about what we watch or listen to on our own. If the parent is listening, however, the child is likely to do so too, even if it is upsetting to them.

Also consider what your family does when you reunite after a day at school or work. What kind of information do you tend to gather from your children? Do they present the problems of the day, or the things they liked most? Try asking them to share something they didn't expect, or the positive aspects of the day instead of just the challenges.

Often as parents we focus on things we think we may need to help our children fix, rather than the success or newness of the day. They may focus on negative information, or we may be asking for it. Either way, be sure to balance these conversations by asking for positive experiences, and then give that information a chance to really sink in.

Finally, what do you do to help relieve your own stress? How do you model taking care of yourself? As many as 70% of couples experience a drop in their enjoyment of their marriage or partnership after becoming parents; and who knows, maybe the other 30% just haven't hit a stressful point yet. Parenting is a very challenging job. The needs of the children are often put first, and parents' needs have to be put on hold. Too often parents are just as sleep deprived as their children, and can't find a way to exercise or do fun and exciting things of their own. Ultimately this is not good for the parents or their children; and it can lead to a decline in physical or mental health, or even marital or relational distress.

It is important to help guide your children by modeling how you take care of yourself. This means finding time for your own self-care—even if you miss some time with the kids. In the long run they will see you managing your stress, and hopefully see you caring for your overall health and well-being. This is what we want for them as well. So the more we do it, the more they will, too.

In the next section, I have included some family activities that you can use to practice these skills together. I hope one of them finds its way into your family.

FAMILY ACTIVITIES

1) Plan to Have No Plans

Take a family outing somewhere without a plan or a specific destination in mind. (This is harder for parents than it is for kids!) Stop when you get to a place that looks interesting and explore something totally new. Afterwards, reflect on what this was like. Sometimes having no expectation of an event removes the fears or frustrations of things not going right. In addition, having a brand new or unexpected experience helps our brain get into information-gathering mode. If you haven't been there or done it before, it's all new!

2) House Cleaning to Treasure Hunt

House cleaning is never fun, but this family activity puts a new spin on cleaning. The goal is to see what new experiences you can have while making a room nice and clean. For example, you could turn a search for misplaced items into a treasure hunt, or rearrange the furniture to create a different feeling to the room. You could also hang up a new family photo, or a piece of art someone in the family made. Most importantly do these activities together and see if you enjoy them better than doing them alone. When you are finished, take some time to explore the room with your family paying attention to things about the room that you never noticed before. Even families who always keep their rooms clean can benefit from this exercise—move things around, hang new art, or hide a few things and see who can find them first.

3) Go on an African Safari

No, you don't need to buy plane tickets for this family activity, but you can use your powerful imagination, can't you? (You can also call it a "walk in the park" or a "hike on a trail" if you like.) Use this time together to noticing things around you. Are there plants you didn't notice before? Has a tree come down that used to be there? What animals can you see or hear? What time of year is it? Can you tell what the animals are up to? See if you can find all the colors of the rainbow while on the safari. Spend time just listening to each other's observations.

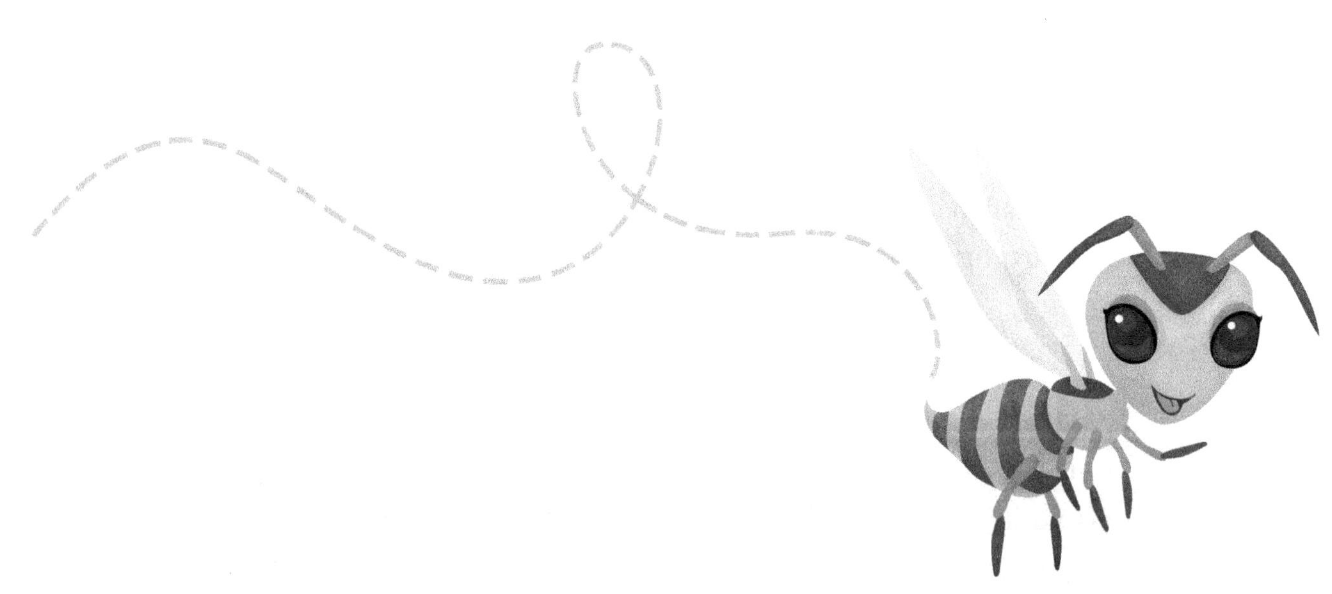

SUMMARY

Using Both the Hornet and the Hippo

Let's go back to the beginning of our workbook where you imagined your own hornet and hippo in your brain. You learned so much about them, and now you understand how important it is to have both of these creatures helping you through a world of new and exciting experiences. I hope you use your hornet any time you need to move to safety, defend yourself, or to push towards an amazing goal. Remember, fear is normal. Try to use that fear only when you really need it.

I also want you to be able to stay curious-and-in-control to help you gather the information you need. In fact, I want you to use your hippo-brain even when your hornet might want to take over.

As you get more and more practice using the feelings of curious-and-in-control, your hippo-brain will grow stronger and stronger, like a muscle in your arm does when you lift weights.

Hopefully you also chose another animal of your own. Your prefrontal cortex animal is helping you in your decisions. Your personal animal will help you know your values, and guide what information you take in. Your animal lives right in the front of your brain, and will be there whenever you need help.

Using all the different parts of your brain will greatly strengthen your learning potential, and make your brain pay attention to what you want to learn or attend to. With practice you can achieve balance, discover more, feel connected to others, understand more, and reach more goals of your very own. When you are able to do this, you will see just how amazing you really are!

MINDFUL
M. E. D. S.
movement   exhale breath   drink water   squat spot
© www.hornets-and-hippos.com

SLEEP CHART

There are so many excellent sleep recommendations out there for parents, that it can often be a challenge to know which to use. Below you will find the sleep chart that I currently use in my clinical practice, which combines guidelines from experts in the fields of pediatrics (inluding the American Academy of Pediatrics, and the Dr. Sears Wellness Institute), as well as my own clinical experience.

CHILD'S AGE	AMOUNT OF SLEEP
Birth to 3 months old	14 to 18 hours
3 to 6 months old	14 to 16 hours
6 months to 2 years old	12 to 14 hours
2 to 3 years old	13 hours
3 to 4 years old	11 to 12 hours
5 years old	11 hours
6 to 8 years old	10 to 11 hours
9 to 10 years old	10 to 12 hours
11 to 12 years old	9 to 11 hours

A NOTE FOR PARENTS

Children who are still napping after five years of age may need slightly less sleep at night. The chart above provides averages—so some children do function well with more, or less, sleep. However, in my clinical experience the more sleep children get, the better. I often suggest that parents add more sleep to the child's daily routine before any other behavioral interventions—just to see if that lowers the number of incidents of the behavioral problems they are trying to address.

If you are concerned that your child is not getting enough sleep, try adding an extra hour to their routine. If they seem happier and more engaged during the day and display fewer incidences of the behavior of concern, then you will know that you are on the right track.

Remember, parents, you need to get your sleep, too! There is nothing like a good night's sleep to fill us with the energy we need to be ready to take on all the new challenges that our children bring. Sleep disruption is seen in almost every mental health condition—so the better we sleep, the better able we are to defend ourselves from mental and physical stress. As adults we sometimes forget we are just big kids with bigger responsibilities and the freedom to parent ourselves.

More Hornets & Hippos

I am so glad that you have read *Hornets & Hippos*. Here are more ways to make the most out of your workbook.

LISTEN TO MINDFULNESS RECORDINGS ON YOUTUBE

The more you practice using mindfulness the easier it will be to feel less anxious and angry. Each of the mindful moments in this workbook have been audio recorded with music to make it even easier for you to practice.

Play them before bed or when you are feeling scared. There will be more added soon, so feel free to subscribe to the channel to recieve notices of any new recordings. Visit the Hornets & Hippos YouTube channel at:

- https://www.youtube.com/channel/UCD6pO-iPaqBOkIB0NDz5tUQ

VISIT THE HORNETS AND HIPPOS WEBSITE

You will find downloads of activity pages and some of the worksheets from the workbook to share with others. Downloads are free and new ones are added a few times a year. Visit:

- www.hornets-and-hippos.com

JOIN THE NEWSLETTER

Want to know about upcoming workshops or other events? Join the newsletter and you will receive information 4–6 times a year via email. Emails are never shared with anyone. You can sign up for the newsletter at:

- http://margaretjessoppsyd.com/hornets-and-hippos/newsletter/

Lastly, if you would like to attend a Hornets and Hippos workshop, or host one in your school or in your community, please visit the **upcoming workshops** page at: www.hornets-and-hippos.com. Or send Dr. Jessop an email at: hornetsandhippos@gmail.com.

GLOSSARY

Amygdala

Name for the part of the brain where the fight-or-flight response is initiated; what this workbook calls the "hornet."

Anxious

Clinical term for fear, or being scared.

Brain Science

The growing body of information on how the brain works, and the effects the brain has on our body and mind.

Breath

The automatic movement of air in and out of our lungs.

Content

Feeling happy, peaceful, and comfortable.

Chemical Messages

Neurotransmitters that send information throughout the brain.

Cortisol

Stress hormone released when we are in the fight-or-flight response.

Cuddle Hormone

Another name for the hormone oxytocin, which is released by the pituitary gland; it plays an important role in relationships and pair bonding.

Curious and In Control

Description of when you are in hippo-mode, using your senses to take in information all around you, and being mindful.

Empathy

The ability to imagine how another feels, and sit with them without expecting the emotion to go away.

Exhale

The part of the breath when you let the air out of your lungs (para sympathetic).

Fear File

A description of the area of the brain where fearful memories and all attached emotions are stored.

Fight-or-Flight

Survival response to real or imagined danger.

Goal

Something you want to accomplish.

Grateful

Being appreciative or thankful of something in your life; noticing the positive.

Heart Rate

The number of heartbeats per minute.

Hippocampus

The name for the part of the brain which we use to take in the context of a situation around us; what this workbook calls the "hippo."

Hippo-brain

What this workbook calls the area of your brain that takes in the context of the situation around you, and then moves that information into storage.

Hippo-mode

What this workbook calls the mode you enter when you use your hippocampus (and all of your senses) to take in the information around you.

Hippo Pond

An activity page included in this workbook to help you gather things you are grateful for.

History File

A description of the area of the brain where memory of events in your life is stored.

Hornet-brain

The part in your brain that helps you identify and react to real or imagined danger.

Hornet's Nest (Hive)

What this workbook calls the strengthening or building up of neurological pathways, which are created by your hornet (amygdala) when you are fearful or angry.

Imagination

The ability to think and create ideas and thoughts in your mind.

Inhale

The part of the breath when you bring air into your lungs (sympathetic).

Mindful M.E.D.S.

An acronym in this workbook that stands for Movement, Exhale, Drink Water, and Squat Spot; used as a technique to calm the fight-or-flight response.

Mindful Moments

Guided meditations geared for a beginner to learn about mindfulness through active practice.

Mindfulness

The practice of focusing your attention on the moment with curiosity.

Negativity Bias

The brain's ability to remember negative or life-threating information more easily than neutral or positive information.

Neuron

A cell in the brain that transmits information.

New, Nice, Natural, or The Three N's

A mindfulness activity included in this workbook that helps you notice new, nice, and natural things everyday.

Overreacting

An emotional reaction that is larger than the situation calls for.

Oxytocin

A hormone released by the pituitary gland in the brain; also called the "cuddle hormone" because it is produced when we get or give hugs.

Prefrontal Cortex

The part of the brain behind the forehead where we make decisions.

S.E.E.D. Parenting

An acronym that is used in this workbook for parenting strategies; it stands for Self Calm, Empathy for Emotion, Emotions to the Body, and Direct with Respect.

Social Learning/Social Referencing

Our ability to watch others and follow what they are doing; often seen when children look to their parent(s) to learn what they should do, or need to be doing.

Squat Spot

What this workbook calls a squatting body movement that helps lower your heart rate. Also can be done seated.

Stable

The feeling of being centered, balanced or grounded.

Survival Mode

A state of body and mind that occurs when you believe your life might be in danger.

Symptoms of Survival Mode

The physical changes that happen when you are in fight-or-flight mode. These include: shallow breathing; increased heart rate; sweating; nausea; urge to use the bathroom; increased energy; thickening of the blood; and blood flow out to the arms and legs.

Thought Pattern

A way of thinking that is often repeated.

Vagus Nerve

The tenth cranial nerve, which interfaces with the parasympathetic control of the heart.

What Fires Together, Wires Together

A term scientists use to describe what happens when neuronal connections in the brain grow stronger as you repeat a behavior or thought pattern; the more you practice, the stronger these connections grow.

OTHER RESOURCES

RELATED CHILDREN'S BOOKS

Deak, JoAnn. *Your Fantastic Elastic Brain: Stretch It, Shape It.* San Francisco, CA: Little Pickle Press, 2013

Snel, Eline. *Sitting Still Like a Frog: Mindfulness Exercises for Kids and Their Parents.* Boston, MA: Shambhala Publications, Inc., 2013

Rubenstein, Lauren. *Visiting Feelings.* Washington, DC: Magination Press, 2014

ARTICLES ON THE INTERNET

Chudler, Eric. "Modeling the nervous system." [Web page]. Retrieved from http://faculty.washington.edu/chudler/chmodel.html

TED TALKS/YOUTUBE VIDEOS

McGonigal, Kelly. "Making stress your friend." [Video]. Retrieved from http://www.ted.com/talks/kelly_mcgonigal_how_to_make_stress_your_friend.html

Hansen, Rick. "Hardwiring Happiness" [Video]. Retrieved from https://www.youtube.com/watch?v=jpuDyGgIeh0

Children Talk about Mindfulness. [Short film]. Retrieved from http://www.mindful.org/news/kindergarteners-talk-about-mindfulness-in-just-breathe-short-film

HELPFUL WEBSITES

Yoga Kids [Website] — http://www.yogakids.com

PHONE APPS

• "3D Brain" by Cold Spring Harbor Laboratory:
Features great visuals of the brain

• "Relax LiteL Stress and Anxiety Relief" by Saagara.
Features breathing prompts for extended exhale

• "Stress Doctor" by Azumio Inc.
Helps teach you breathing strategies for feeling calm

BIBLIOGRAPHY

American Academy of Pediatrics. (2016) "American Academy of Pediatrics Supports Childhood Sleep Guidelines." [Web page]. Retrieved from https://www.aap.org/en-us/about-the-aap/aap-press-room/pages/American-Academy-of-Pediatrics-Supports-Childhood-Sleep-Guidelines.aspx

Buchanan, T.W. & Preston, S.D. (2014) "Stress leads to prosocial action in immediate need situations." *Frontiers in Behavioral Neuroscience*, Vol. 8 (5), 1-6.

Doidge, Norman. *The Brain that Changes Itself: Stories of Personal Triumph from the Frontiers of Brain Science*. New York: Penguin Books, 2007

Flynn, Lisa. *Yoga for Children: 200 Yoga Poses, Breathing Exercises, and Meditations for Healthier, Happier, More Resilient Children*. Avon, Massachusetts: Adams Media, 2013

Gopnik, Alison. *The Philosophical Baby: What Children's Minds Tell Us About Truth, Love, and the Meaning of Life*. New York: Farrar, Straus and Giroux, 2009

Gottman, John and J. Gottman. *And Baby Makes Three: The Six-Step Plan for Preserving Marital Intimacy and Rekindling Romance After Baby Arrives*. New York: Three Rivers Press, 2007

Hanson, Rick and R. Mendius. *Buddha's Brain: Happiness, Love and Wisdom*. Oakland: New Harbinger Publication, Inc., 2009

Hanson, Rick. *Hardwiring Happiness: The New Brain Science of Contentment, Calm, and Confidence*. New York: Harmony Books, 2013

Keller, A., Litzelman, K., Wisk, L. E., Maddox, T., Cheng, E. R., Creswell, P. D., Witt, W. P. (2012) "Does the perception that stress affects health matter? The association with health and mortality." Health Psychology, Vol. 31 (5), 677-684.

Kornfield, Jack, and D. Siegel. *Mindfulness and the Brain: A Professional Training in the Science and Practice of Meditative Awareness*. [Audio Book]. Sounds True, September 2011

Medina, John. *Brain Rules for Baby: How to Raise a Smart and Happy Child from Zero to Five*. Seattle, WA: Pear Press, 2010

Metzl, Jordan D. *The Exercise Cure: A Doctor's All-Natural No-Pill Prescription for Better Health and Longer Life*. New York, NY: Rodale Inc., 2013

Rama, Swami. *Meditation and Its Practice*. Honesdale, Pennsylvania: Himalayan Institute, 2012

Sears, Willam M.D., and M. Sears. "How Much Sleep Should Your Child Get Each Night." [Web page]. Retrieved from https://www.askdrsears.com/topics/health-concerns/sleep-problems/faqs-about-sleep-problems/how-much-sleep

Siegel, Daniel J. and T. Payne Bryson. *The Whole-Brain Child: Twelve Revolutionary Strategies to Nurture Your Child's Developing Mind*. New York: Bantam Books Trade Paperbacks, 2011

Teper, R., Segal, Z.V. & Inzlicht, M. (2013). "Inside the mindful mind: How mindfulness enhances emotion regulation through improvements in executive control." *Association for Psychological Science* 22(6) 449-454.

Weontraub, Amy. *Yoga Skills for Therapists*. New York: W. W. Norton & Company, 2012